Cat and Cat Comics

THE WORLD ACCORDING TO CATS

A GUIDE TO FELINE FEELINGS

A STUDIO PRESS BOOK

First published in the UK in 2020 by Studio Press,
an imprint of Bonnier Books UK,
The Plaza, 535 King's Road, London SW10 0SZ
Owned by Bonnier Books, Sveavägen 56, Stockholm, Sweden

www.studiopressbooks.co.uk
www.bonnierbooks.co.uk

1 3 5 7 9 10 8 6 4 2
ISBN 978-17874-1-954-4

MIX
Paper from
responsible sources
FSC® C104723
FSC
www.fsc.org

Written by Susie Yi
Edited by Stephanie Milton and Laura Pollard
Designed by Nia Williams

@catandcatcomics

A CIP catalogue for this book is available from the British Library
Printed and bound in China

Cat and Cat Comics
THE WORLD ACCORDING TO CATS

STUDIO
PRESS

Thank you to my patrons, especially Mimi, David Brooks, Max Power, Janna Laverdiere, and Chippy Fernando. I am also grateful to my webcomics group, and Beanie and Guy for the unending love and support throughout. Finally, thank you to all my readers from the bottom of my heart. I appreciate all of you!

Cat and Cat comics is a cosy comic about life lessons, designed to make you laugh, cry and generally improve your day. Whether you're a cat lover or not, these comics give glimpses into the lives of pets that will surely make you smile! These comics are partly based on the antics of Mickey and Minnie, two rescue cats who love to run around, sleep in random places and enjoy their lives basking in the sun by the window.

CAT LOVE

Cats have a habit of showing love in strange ways. We may not always understand their displays of affection or why they do what they do, but deep down, they love us very much!

CAT DEMANDS

When cats want something, they must have it immediately! Whether it's late night entertainment or finding the perfect lunch, we'll do anything to keep them happy and satisfied.

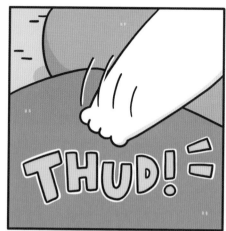

CAT JUDGEMENT

No one judges us quite like our cats. They see us at our best and our worst, and they're not afraid to dish out some tough love! They like to keep us on our toes.

CAT SCHEDULES

A day in the life of a cat is a very busy one indeed. Cats like to operate on a schedule, whether they're doing very important work or letting loose and having fun. It's a finely tuned system!

A long day of work for both human and cats.

CAT WISDOM

During their nine lifetimes, cats learn plenty of excellent life lessons. The next time your cat is meowing at you, consider listening to their sage advice!

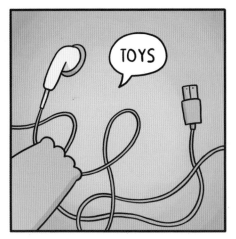

CAT EGO

At the end of the day, cats know that they're the most important creatures on the planet, and they want to make sure that we know it, too! From their physical prowess to their mental acumen, cats know they are simply the best.

The clock strikes midnight.

The hero jumps to action!

AND FALLS!

THWACK!!!!!

. . .

...no one saw that.

FWIP

CAT GRATITUDE

Cats show gratitude in ways that we humans sometimes can't understand! They may be kneading your tummy with their sharp claws, but cats would like to reassure you that it's because they are truly thankful for everything you do.

CAT PHYSICS

Introducing the Law of
Catodynamics, where everything
we thought we knew about
science changes! Cats are a law
unto themselves, and they will
defy the laws of human physics.

RANDOM CAT BEDS!

THE SINK

A LAPTOP

WARM, FRESH PIZZA

ON YOUR HEAD

Chocolate
Doughnut

Jelly
Doughnut

Blueberry
Doughnut

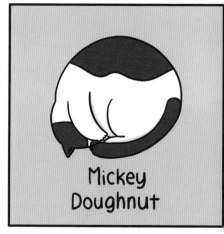

Mickey
Doughnut

CAT RELATIONSHIPS

Cats interact with each other in curious ways, and, much like human relationships, every relationship is unique. We only see what's on the surface, and that's how they want to keep it.